Under, Over, By the Clover

What Is a Preposition?

To Patrick, Clare, Fiona, and Luke,
who are BEYOND good. —B.P.C.

To the indomitable Spot
—B.G.

Preposition: A word that connects a noun or pronoun to other words in a sentence.

Under, Over, By the Clover

What Is a Preposition?

by Brian P. Cleary

illustrated by Brian Gable

M MILLBROOK PRESS / MINNEAPOLIS

beside the chair—

under,

over,

by the

clover,

About,
above,
or next to
Rover.

They tell us

time and also place,

During recess

after school,

in
between
the pond
and pool.

Ever since the olden days, there's been a silly myth

That
prepositions
aren't correct
to end a sentence with.

But write your sentence carefully,
and you'll discover that

Ending
with a
preposition

is often where it's **at**.

Prepositions give direction

Like, doctors rushed
to Rhonda's wrecked shin.

Or charlie danced
the charleston
over on the green,

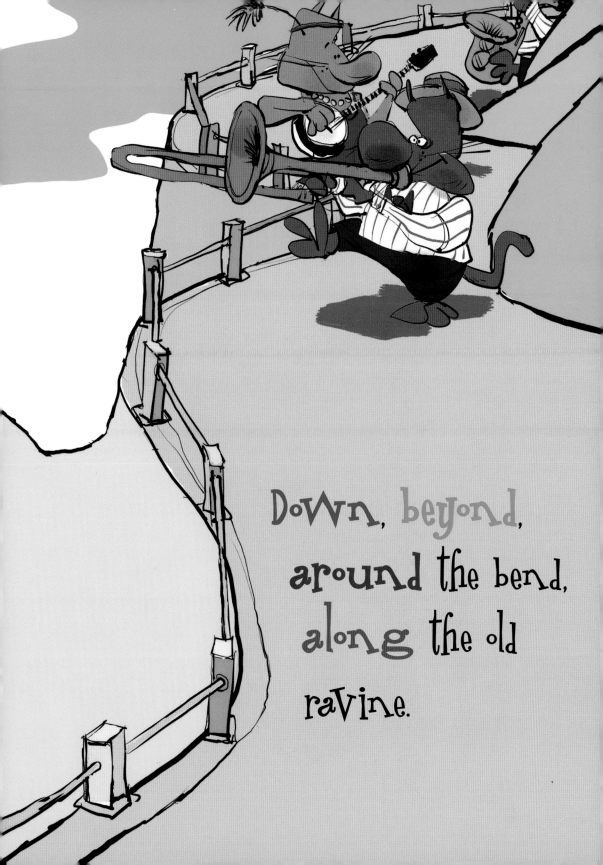

Down, beyond,
around the bend,
along the old
raVine.

Across
the way,

toward

Mississippi,

Through
the yard
of Chris, the hippie.

Like, Paul's from Pittsburgh,

Way up there,

I hid beneath
the old oak chair—

Into, inside,
from the zoo,

Home by way
of Timbuktu.

They tell the
whens, the wheres,
the hows,

'cause that's
their special
mission,
and help to link
the other words—

That's what's a preposition!

So, what is a
Preposition?
Do you know?

About the Author & Illustrator

BRIAN P. CLEARY is the author of the best-selling Words Are CATegorical© series, as well as the Math Is CATegorical©, Food Is CATegorical™, Animal Groups Are CATegorical™, Adventures in Memory™, and Sounds Like Reading© series. He has also written Do You Know Dewey? Exploring the Dewey Decimal System, Six Sheep Sip Thick Shakes: And Other Tricky Tongue Twisters, and several other books. Mr. Cleary lives in Cleveland, Ohio.

BRIAN GABLE is the illustrator of many Words Are CATegorical© books and the Math Is CATegorical© series. Mr. Gable also works as a political cartoonist for the Globe and Mail newspaper in Toronto, Canada.

This book is available in two editions:
Library binding by Millbrook Press, a division of Lerner Publishing Group, Inc.
Soft cover by First Avenue Editions, an imprint of Lerner Publishing Group, Inc.
241 First Avenue North, Minneapolis, MN 55401 USA

For reading levels and more information, look up this title at www.lernerbooks.com.

Library of Congress Cataloging-in-Publication Data

Cleary, Brian P., 1959—
   Under, over, by the clover : what is a preposition? / by Brian P.
Cleary ; illustrated by Brian Gable.
   p.   cm. — (Words are categorical)
   ISBN 978-1-57505-524-4 (lib. bdg. : alk. paper)
   ISBN 978-1-57505-201-4 (pbk. : alk. paper)
   ISBN 978-1-57505-570-1 (EB pdf)
1. English language—Prepositions—Juvenile literature. [1. English
language—Prepositions.] I. Gable, Brian, 1949– ill. II. Title.
PE1335.C581 2002
428.2—dc21   2001001263

Manufactured in China
10-41674-7342-3/23/2016